ROCK & ROI

TRIVIA QUIZ BOOK

VOLUME 3

400 ROCK TRIVIA QUESTIONS
(1970s–1980s)

*an encyclopedia of rock & roll's
trivia-information

in question/answer format*

Copyright © 2018 by:
Raymond Karelitz
Hi-Lite Publishing Company
Rock-&-Roll Test Prep Hawaii
P.O. Box 6071
Kaneohe, Hawaii 96744

email comments/corrections: rocktrivia@test-prepHi.com
(808) 261-6666

VOLUME 1-- Updated 2019 ed.

Love, Presley

ROCK & ROLL TRIVIA QUIZ BOOK Vol. 1
(128 pages)

1. Rock-&-Roll Quiz Book   I. Love, Presley   II. Title: Rock and Roll

2. Music

COVER DESIGN: *Doug Behrens*

ISBN: 978-1984962584

Printed In The United States of America

----

text collection by: **Presley Love**
format/production by: Raymond Karelitz

The Legacy of Presley Love

In 1992, music-aficionado Presley Love compiled a vast treasure of rock & roll lyric-memoribilia, including songs from the earliest days of rock & roll up through the late '80s. This musical quiz-format collection lay dormant except for the release of a single volume which contained 400 questions. The original book — printed in 1992 — became, over the years, an Amazon.com favorite, with very positive response from those who loved the book for its "party-flavor" appeal.

In 2014, the entire vault of Presley Love's music-lyric memoribilia was located in a storage locker — containing his collection of lyric-questions and trivia questions in quiz format! After four years of diligent compiling and organizing, the entire Presley Love collection of rock lyrics, rock titles and rock group trivia is now available in quiz-format!

We are proud to unveil the exciting 4-volume set of Presley Love's *ROCK TRIVIA QUIZ BOOKS 1970s-1980s,* including amazing and little-known facts from the rock era of the '70s & '80s. We hope you enjoy these fabulous party-favorites in quiz-format, books guaranteed to amuse, entertain and inform!

If you're brave enough to test your skills,
here's a simple SCORING CHART:

(questions are worth 1 point each — "Harder Questions" are worth 2 points each . . . If you are able to correctly answer the question without the three choices, you receive twice the point value!)

If you score . . .

20+ Points: You probably STILL think it's 1975!
(Check your wardrobe!)

16–19: You probably paid more attention to rock & roll than books & school!
(Check your report card!)

11–15: There's a lot of rock & roll memories in your blood!

6–10: Don't you wish you'd listened more closely to rock & roll ?!
(It's never too late to be hip!)

0–5: Where were YOU when rock began to rule ?!
(Time to get experienced —
run to your music store now!!!)

ROCK TRIVIA QUESTIONS

Quiz 1

1. After their breakup in 1970, which former Beatle was the first to tour America ?
   a. George Harrison
   b. Paul McCartney
   c. John Lennon

****

2. What is the relationship between the groups Malo and Santana ?
   a. Malo was the band that later became Santana
   b. both Latino groups had a U.S. #1 hit in 1972
   c. the leaders of both bands are brothers

****

3. Which of the following songs initially was endorsed by a branch of the armed forces, but later un-endorsed ?
   a. *Fortunate Son*
   b. *The Ballad of the Green Berets*
   c. *In the Navy*

****

4. Why did *Layla,* a smash hit in 1972 by Derek & the Dominoes, not even reach the Top 40 when it was first released ?
   a. it was released on a lesser-known record label
   b. it lacked the quality of the later recording
   c. nobody knew that it featured Eric Clapton

5. Who was another artist besides composer Randy Newman to record *Mama Told Me (Not to Come)* prior to the 1970 #1 release by Three Dog Night ?

      a. Eric Burdon

      b. Tom Jones

      c. Otis Redding

****

6. What was the name of Frank Zappa's offbeat backup band of the '60s and '70s ?

      a. the GTO's

      b. the Nazz

      c. the Mothers of Invention

****

7. Who helped contribute background vocals in Ringo Starr's 1971 hit *It Don't Come Easy*?

      a. David Crosby

      b. Stephen Stills

      c. Graham Nash

****

8. Who won the Grammy for Best New Artist of the Year for 1971?

      a. Elton John

      b. Rod Stewart

      c. Carly Simon

9. On which label did Stevie Wonder record his biggest hits, including *Higher Ground* ?

   a. Tamla
   b. Philles
   c. Philly International

****

10. What was Elton John songwriter Bernie Taupin's real (birth) name ?

   a. Leland Smythe
   b. Market Rasen
   c. Ethan McIntyre

****

Questions 11-16: **SONG HITS**

11. What was the Staple Singers' first U.S. Billboard Top 20 hit ?

   a. *If You're Ready (Come Go With Me)*
   b. *Respect Yourself*
   c. *I'll Take You There*

****

12. What was Billy Preston's first U.S. Billboard Top 40 hit ?

   a. *Outa-Space*
   b. *Space Race*
   c. *Will It Go Round In Circles*

13. Which of the following hits charted highest for Bread on the U.S. Billboard singles chart ?

      a. *If*

      b. *Make It With You*

      c. *Baby I'm-A Want You*

****

14. What was Rod Stewart's first solo hit single to reach the U.S. Billboard Top 20 record charts ?

      a. *You Wear It Well*

      b. *Maggie May*

      c. *You're In My Heart*

****

15. What was the Grateful Dead's only Top 20 song ?

      a. *Touch of Grey*

      b. *Truckin'*

      c. *Casey Jones*

****

16. Which of the following #1 hits charted the longest for Three Dog Night on the U.S. singles chart ?

      a. *Joy to the World*

      b. *Black & White*

      c. *Mama Told Me (Not to Come)*

17. What group did Tony Burrows NOT sing lead for ?

    a. White Plains

    b. the First Class

    c. Edison Lighthouse

****

18. What group did Left Banke leader Michael Brown form in 1971?

    a. Brownsville Station

    b. the Five Man Electrical Band

    c. Stories

****

19. What was Badfinger known as when they first signed to Apple Records ?

    a. the Iveys

    b. the Bad Apples

    c. the West Side Four

****

20. Who said the following in a radio interview, reflecting upon his own recording career: "I enjoyed doing it . . . it was not like I had stage-parents who shoved me into something I didn't want to do . . . If it was, then I don't think I could have made it this long . . . I would have probably overdosed or something . . ."

    a. Donny Osmond

    b. Rick Nelson

    c. Michael Jackson

answers

Quiz 1

1. a. George Harrison, in 1974, though his concerts were barely half-filled with fans . . . John Lennon's first tour fared with greater success a few months later
2. c. the leaders of both bands are brothers (Malo was formed by Jorge Santana, brother of Carlos Santana)
3. c. *In the Navy,* 1979 hit by the Village People — the lyrics, by the way, were very Navy-friendly!
4. c. nobody knew that it featured Eric Clapton . . . once word spread upon its re-release that Eric Clapton was lead singer/guitarist, *Layla* quickly became a Top 20 hit
5. a. Eric Burdon
6. c. the Mothers of Invention
7. b. Stephen Stills
8. c. Carly Simon
9. a. Tamla
10. b. Market Rasen

****

Questions 11-16: SONG HITS

11. b. *Respect Yourself*
12. a. *Outa-Space*
13. b. *Make It With You,* #1 in 1970
14. b. *Maggie May,* in 1971
15. a. *Touch of Grey* . . . not in the '60s, or even in the '70s . . . it happened in 1987!
16. a. *Joy to the World,* #1 for 6 weeks in 1971

****

Questions 17-20: HARDER QUESTIONS

17. b. the First Class . . . he did also sing lead for the Brotherhood of Man
18. c. Stories, whose 1973 hit *Brother Louie* was a million-seller
19. a. the Iveys
20. c. Michael Jackson

Quiz 2

1. Where did Bachman–Turner Overdrive get the name "Overdrive" from ?
   - a. a truckers' magazine
   - b. their over–the–top live performances
   - c. a random word chosen from the dictionary

****

2. Three Dog Night had a U.S. #1 hit in 1972 with *Black and White.* What British group released the song one year earlier ?
   - a. Middle of the Road
   - b. Greyhound
   - c. Atomic Rooster

****

3. Which Rolling Stones album featured an Andy Warhol cover including a real zipper ?
   - a. *Between the Buttons*
   - b. *Get Yer Ya–Ya's Out*
   - c. *Sticky Fingers*

****

4. Who was the actual subject of the Nitty Gritty Dirt Band's 1971 hit *Mr. Bojangles* ?
   - a. a fellow cell–mate
   - b. a character from a Dr. Seuss book
   - c. Bill "Bojangles" Robinson

5. According to the Billboard Hot 100 singles chart, what was the most successful song for Bell Records during the '70s ?

    a. *Tie a Yellow Ribbon Round the Ole Oak Tree*

    b. *Seasons In the Sun*

    c. *The Night the Lights Went Out In Georgia*

****

6. What was the name of the newly-formed group after the Yardbirds broke up, prior to the renaming of the new group as Led Zeppelin ?

    a. Heavy Metal Thunder

    b. the New Yardbirds

    c. the Bluesbreakers

****

7. Which million-selling single never cracked the Hot 100 Billboard charts for Elton John ?

    a. *Candle in the Wind*

    b. *Step Into Christmas*

    c. *Your Song*

****

8. Which single won a Grammy for Record of the Year for 1972 ?

    a. *American Pie*

    b. *Alone Again (Naturally)*

    c. *The First Time Ever I Saw Your Face*

9. Which group featured members including Denny, Justin, Mike and Graeme ?

      a. the Moody Blues

      b. Wings

      c. Argent

****

10. Who was Mariska Veres the lead singer for ?

      a. the Tee Set

      b. Shocking Blue

      c. the Flying Machine

****

Questions 11-16: SONG HITS

11. According to Billboard's Hot 100 singles chart, what was the #1 song for 1972 ?

      a. *American Pie*

      b. *Alone Again (Naturally)*

      c. *The First Time Ever I Saw Your Face*

****

12. What was Dawn's last U.S. Top 20 hit ?

      a. *Mornin' Beautiful*

      b. *He Don't Love You (Like I Love You)*

      c. *Look In My Eyes Pretty Woman*

13. What was the Bee Gees' first #1 U.S. Billboard #1 hit ?

    a. *Jive Talkin'*

    b. *You Should Be Dancing*

    c. *How Can You Mend a Broken Heart*

****

14. What was the Stylistics' first U.S. Billboard Top 20 hit ?

    a. *Betcha By Golly, Wow*

    b. *You Are Everything*

    c. *I'm Stone In Love With You*

****

15. What was Bobby Sherman's last U.S. Top 40 hit ?

    a. *Easy Come, Easy Go*

    b. *Julie, Do Ya Love Me*

    c. *Cried Like a Baby*

****

16. Which of the following hits charted highest for Carly Simon on the U.S. Billboard singles chart ?

    a. *Nobody Does It Better*

    b. *You Belong to Me*

    c. *You're So Vain*

17. Which '70s rock group was Yardbirds' lead
    singer Keith Relf NOT a member of ?

> a. Armageddon
> b. Renaissance
> c. the Mob

****

18. On what TV show did Led Zeppelin make its U.S.
    debut ?

> a. *The Midnight Special*
> b. *Don Kirschner's Rock Concert*
> c. *The Sonny and Cher Show*

****

19. Who was Susan (referred to in the song as
    "Suzanne") in James Taylor's factually reflective
    Fire & Rain ?

> a. a 3rd–grade childhood sweetheart
> b. his first wife
> c. a woman he met in a mental institution

****

20. What inspired calling the '70s band "Bread" ?

> a. it was a humorous comment on what they
>   weren't earning any of
> b. the group got stuck behind a bread truck
> c. it was leader David Gates' favorite food

Quiz 2

1. a. a truckers' magazine titled *Overdrive*
2. b. Greyhound, reaching #6 in 1971
3. c. *Sticky Fingers*
4. a. a fellow cell-mate ... Writer Jerry Jeff Walker recounted a brief stint
   in a county jail, where he met an intriguing has-been drunkard who had
   in the past been a minstrel show dancer known as "Mr. Bojangles"
5. a. *Tie a Yellow Ribbon Round the Ole Oak Tree,* by Dawn
6. b. the New Yardbirds
7. b. *Step Into Christmas* . . . though it has gained popularity
   over the years — notably during Christmastime — it was
   originally released towards the end of the holiday season
   in 1973, diminishing its immediate popularity
8. c. *The First Time Ever I Saw Your Face,* by Roberta Flack
9. a. the Moody Blues
10. b. Shocking Blue

****

Questions 11-16: SONG HITS

11. a. *American Pie,* by Don McLean
12. a. *Mornin' Beautiful*
13. c. *How Can You Mend a Broken Heart,* in 1971
14. b. *You Are Everything*
15. c. *Cried Like a Baby*
16. c. *You're So Vain,* #1 for 3 weeks in 1973

****

Questions 17-20: HARDER QUESTIONS

17. c. the Mob
18. b. *Don Kirschner's Rock Concert,* in which they played *Black Dog*
19. c. a woman he met in a mental institution . . . Afraid that he
    himself was losing his mind, Taylor admitted himself to a
    mental hospital, where he met Susan. The song is a reflection
    of what could have been had she not shortly thereafter
    committed suicide.
20. b. the group got caught in traffic, stuck behind a Wonder Bread
    truck

Quiz 3

1. Which of the following groups was Byrds drummer Michael Clarke NOT later a member of ?
   - a. the Flying Burrito Brothers
   - b. Poco
   - c. Firefall

****

2. What separated David Bowie from other male performers in his '70s concerts ?
   - a. he sang in a high falsetto voice
   - b. he had no musical backup band
   - c. he often wore dresses

****

3. Before they became 10cc, the group (then a trio, later to add a fourth member and become 10cc) had a Top 40 U.S. Hit (Top 5 in the U.K). What was this hit ?
   - a. *Hot Love*
   - b. *Run Run Run*
   - c. *Neanderthal Man*

****

4. What unusual physical characteristic has made Edgar Winter unique in rock & roll ?
   - a. he is 6'11", the tallest rocker
   - b. he has six fingers on one hand
   - c. he is albino

5. Which vocal group — initially consisting of three brothers whose ages were 3, 4 & 5 years old — toured along with their mother, singing gospel songs in churches throughout Ohio and Kentucky ?

        a. the Isley Brothers

        b. the Jackson 5

        c. the Osmonds

****

6. General Johnson was the lead singer of what group ?

        a. Chairmen of the Board

        b. the Undisputed Truth

        c. the Dramatics

****

7. Which song by Three Dog Night was originally written for a children's animated television special ?

        a. *Black and White*

        b. *Joy to the World*

        c. *Celebrate*

****

8. Who won the Grammy for Best New Artist of the Year for 1970 ?

        a. James Taylor

        b. Badfinger

        c. the Carpenters

9. Which group featured members including John, John Paul, Robert and Jimmy ?

        a. Led Zeppelin

        b. Black Sabbath

        c. Manfred Mann's Earth Band

****

10. On which label did Badfinger record their hits, including *Come and Get It* ?

        a. London

        b. Apple

        c. Rare Earth

****

Questions 11-16: SONG HITS

11. What was David Cassidy's last U.S. Top 40 hit ?

        a. *Rock Me Baby*

        b. *How Can I Be Sure*

        c. *Could It Be Forever*

****

12. What was Anne Murray's first U.S. Billboard Top 40 hit ?

        a. *You Needed Me*

        b. *Snowbird*

        c. *Danny's Song*

13. Which of the following hits charted highest for Billy Preston on the U.S. Billboard singles chart ?

       a. *Outa-Space*

       b. *Nothing From Nothing*

       c. *Will It Go Round In Circles*

****

14. What was Cat Stevens' first single to reach the U.S. Billboard Top 20 record charts ?

       a. *Morning Has Broken*

       b. *Peace Train*

       c. *Wild World*

****

15. What was Johnny Nash's only U.S. #1 hit ?

       a. *Hold Me Tight*

       b. *Stir It Up*

       c. *I Can See Clearly Now*

****

16. What was George Harrison's first U.S. Billboard Top 40 hit ?

       a. *Give Me Love (Give Me Peace On Earth)*

       b. *My Sweet Lord*

       c. *What Is Life ?*

HARDER QUESTIONS (17-20): 2 points each
(4 points if you can answer the question without the three choices !)

17. Which group's members suggested the name
Led Zeppelin ?
> a. the Who
> b. the Yardbirds
> c. Cream

****

18. Who was Elton John's *Daniel* originally written
about ?
> a. a Viet Nam veteran
> b. Elton John's drummer, Nigel Olsson
> c. Danny Thomas

****

19. One of the first two bands signed to the Beach
Boys new Brother Records label was Redwood.
When they left the label, they changed their name.
Who did they then become ?
> a. Three Dog Night
> b. the Grass Roots
> c. Grand Funk Railroad

****

20. What was the actual subject inspiring Neil
Diamond's 1970 hit *Cracklin' Rosie* ?
> a. a girl he knew in the first grade
> b. a bottle of wine
> c. a campfire memory

answers

Quiz 3

1. b. Poco
2. c. he often wore dresses
3. c. *Neanderthal Man,* as Hotlegs
4. c. he is albino, as is his brother Johnny
5. a. the Isley brothers
6. a. Chairmen of the Board
7. b. *Joy to the World,* written for the children's television special *The Happy Song*
8. c. the Carpenters
9. a. Led Zeppelin
10. b. Apple

****

Questions 11-16: SONG HITS

11. a. *Rock Me Baby*
12. b. *Snowbird*
13. c. *Will It Go Round In Circles,* #1 for 2 weeks in 1973
14. c. *Wild World,* in April, 1971
15. c. *I Can See Clearly Now*
16. b. *My Sweet Lord*

****

Questions 17-20: HARDER QUESTIONS

17. a. the Who . . . members Keith Moon and John Entwistle thought that a supergroup with members like Jimmy Page and Steve Winwood would, in one of Moon's pet phrases for a musical disaster, go "down like a lead Zeppelin"
18. a. a Viet Nam veteran . . . Writer Bernie Taupin was inspired by an article in *Newsweek* and wrote a tribute to the man it described as fleeing from the lingering memories of the war.
19. a. Three Dog Night
20. b. a bottle of rose wine that would often serve as a substitute on cold nights when there was no woman around for a man to spend the time with

Quiz 4

1. In what Jackson 5 song did Michael Jackson's final line contain a semantic error ?
   - a. *The Love You Save*
   - b. *I'll Be There*
   - c. *I Want You Back*

****

2. In what country was Stealer's Wheel leader Gerry Rafferty born ?
   - a. Scotland
   - b. New Zealand
   - c. Ireland

****

3. Which of the following was NOT an inspiration for James Taylor's 1970 hit *Fire and Rain* ?
   - a. a friend's suicide
   - b. his own heroin habit
   - c. the Viet Nam war

****

4. Who played piano on the Hollies' hit *He Ain't Heavy, He's My Brother* ?
   - a. Billy Joel
   - b. Neil Sedaka
   - c. Elton John

5. Who produced Grand Funk Railroad's first #1 hit, *We're An American Band*?

> **a.** Bruce Springsteen
>
> **b.** Todd Rundgren
>
> **c.** Kenny Loggins

****

6. What name did Alice Cooper briefly use for his band before noticing that it was already the name of a band?

> **a.** the Kiss
>
> **b.** the G.T.O.'s
>
> **c.** the Nazz

****

7. From what did the '70s band America derive their name?

> **a.** from the national anthem
>
> **b.** from a steamroller
>
> **c.** from a jukebox

****

8. Who won the Grammy for Best New Artist of the Year for 1972?

> **a.** the Stylistics
>
> **b.** America
>
> **c.** the Eagles

9. On which label did Jim Croce record his hits, including *Operator*?

> a. RCA
>
> b. ABC
>
> c. MGM

****

10. Which group featured members including Michael, Jeff and Patrick ?

> a. the Doobie Brothers
>
> b. Chicago
>
> c. King Harvest

****

Questions 11-16: SONG HITS

11. What was Elton John's first U.S. Billboard Top 40 hit ?

> a. *Your Song*
>
> b. *Friends*
>
> c. *Levon*

****

12. What was the Eagles' last U.S. Top 40 hit ?

> a. *Seven Bridges Road*
>
> b. *I Can't Tell You Why*
>
> c. *The Long Run*

13. Which of the following hits charted highest for America on the U.S. Billboard singles chart ?

      a. *Sister Golden Hair*

      b. *Ventura Highway*

      c. *A Horse With No Name*

****

14. What was the Doobie Brothers' first single to reach the U.S. Billboard Top 20 record charts ?

      a. *Long Train Running*

      b. *Listen to the Music*

      c. *China Grove*

****

15. What was Bad Company's last U.S. Top 40 hit ?

      a. *Young Blood*

      b. *Rock 'n' Roll Fantasy*

      c. *Feel Like Makin' Love*

****

16. What was the Partridge Family's first U.S. Billboard Top 40 hit ?

      a. *I'll Meet You Halfway*

      b. *I Think I Love You*

      c. *Doesn't Somebody Want to Be Wanted*

17. What was the original title for John Denver's composition *Leaving On A Jet Plane* ?

> a. *Don't Know When I'll Be Back Again*
>
> b. *I'm Ready to Go*
>
> c. *Babe, I Hate to Go*

****

18. The #1 hit *Killing Me Softly With His Song* was originally inspired by the performance of what singer ?

> a. Don McLean
>
> b. Jimmy Buffett
>
> c. Engelbert Humperdinck

****

19. What did '70s supergroup War call themselves prior to their stardom years ?

> a. Hard Luck
>
> b. the Plain Cool Ones
>
> c. the Night Shift

****

20. What song reportedly inspired George Harrison's *My Sweet Lord* ?

> a. *Oh Happy Day*
>
> b. *He's So Fine*
>
> c. *Badge*

Quiz 4

1. b. *I'll Be There,* with the line "just look over your shoulders, honey" . . . young Michael didn't realize that a person can't simultaneously look over both shoulders, but the producer nonetheless chose to keep the cute faux pas intact
2. a. Scotland
3. c. the Viet Nam war
4. c. Elton John
5. b. Todd Rundgren
6. c. the Nazz . . . Todd Rundgren's already-named group Nazz had no affiliation with Cooper
7. c. from a jukebox, which was brand-labeled *An Americana*
8. b. America
9. b. ABC
10. a. the Doobie Brothers

****

Questions 11-16: SONG HITS

11. a. *Your Song,* in 1971
12. a. *Seven Bridges Road*
13. c. *A Horse With No Name,* #1 for 3 weeks in 1972
14. b. *Listen to the Music,* in 1972
15. b. *Rock 'n' Roll Fantasy*
16. b. *I Think I Love You*

****

Questions 17-20: HARDER QUESTIONS

17. c. *Babe, I Hate to Go*
18. a. Don McLean
19. c. the Night Shift
20. a. the Edwin Hawkins Singers' 1969 hit *Oh Happy Day* . . . (lawyers thought differently, however)

Quiz 5

1. Who was the first former Beatle to release a solo recording ?

   a. George Harrison

   b. Paul McCartney

   c. John Lennon

****

2. Which recording artist did Stevie Wonder originally write his 1973 hit *Superstition* for ?

   a. Elton John

   b. Edwin Starr

   c. Jeff Beck

****

3. Who produced Lou Reed's first solo album — containing his 1973 hit *Walk on the Wild Side* ?

   a. Todd Rundgren

   b. David Bowie

   c. Ric Ocasek

****

4. Todd Rundgren's most successful single was his 1973 release of which song recorded by his band, Nazz, in 1969 ?

   a. *I Saw the Light*

   b. *Hello It's Me*

   c. *We Gotta Get You a Woman*

5. Which of the following groups was NOT from Holland ?

        a. Sweet Sensation

        b. Golden Earring

        c. Shocking Blue

****

6. The Allman Brothers Band was the first group to record under a new Atlantic record label. What was the name of the label ?

        a. Arista

        b. Capricorn

        c. Chrysalis

****

7. Which song did Jackson Browne co-write with Glenn Frey, later to become the Eagles' first Top 20 hit ?

        a. *Take it Easy*

        b. *Witchy Woman*

        c. *Lyin' Eyes*

****

8. Which group featured members including Bjorn, Agnetha, Frida and Benny ?

        a. Abba

        b. Blue Swede

        c. Shocking Blue

9. Which famous ballad singer was born Roberta Streeter ?

> a. Roberta Flack
>
> b. Bobbie Gentry
>
> c. Gladys Knight

****

10. What RCA-distributed label did Jefferson Airplane record under, beginning in 1971?

> a. Bark
>
> b. Tetragrammaton
>
> c. Grunt

****

Questions 11-16: SONG HITS

11. What was Neil Diamond's first U.S. #1 hit ?

> a. *I Am . . . I Said*
>
> b. *Cracklin' Rosie*
>
> c. *Song Sung Blue*

****

12. What was John Denver's first U.S. Billboard Top 40 hit ?

> a. *Take Me Home, Country Roads*
>
> b. *Sunshine On My Shoulders*
>
> c. *Rocky Mountain High*

13. What was Gordon Lightfoot's last U.S. Top 20 hit ?

   a. *The Wreck of the Edmund Fitzgerald*

   b. *Sundown*

   c. *Carefree Highway*

****

14. What was the only Led Zeppelin song to break into the U.S. Top 10 singles chart ?

   a. *D'Yer Maker*

   b. *Stairway to Heaven*

   c. *Whole Lotta Love*

****

15. What was Creedence Clearwater Revival's last U.S. Top 40 hit ?

   a. *Sweet Hitch-Hiker*

   b. *Have You Ever Seen the Rain*

   c. *Someday Never Comes*

****

16. What was the Doobie Brothers' first U.S. #1 hit ?

   a. *Long Train Runnin'*

   b. *Black Water*

   c. *What a Fool Believes*

HARDER QUESTIONS (17-20): 2 points each
(4 points if you can answer the question without the three choices !)

17. What '70s group did a member of the '60s *Bend Me Shape Me* American Breed later help form ?

 a. Stealer's Wheel

 b. Rufus

 c. Black Sabbath

****

18. What was the original title of the song that Gladys Knight & the Pips took to the top of the singles chart in 1973 as *Midnight Train to Georgia*?

 a. *Midnight Plane to Houston*

 b. *Mid-day Cruise to Jamaica*

 c. *Midnight Train to Tulsa*

****

19. Just prior to signing with Warner Brothers Records, what did the rock-trio group America call themselves ?

 a. Triad

 b. Soldiers of Rock

 c. A Group With No Name

****

20. Which song won the 1972 Grammy award for Best R&B (Rhythm & Blues) Instrumental ?

 a. *Scorpio*

 b. *Joy*

 c. *Papa Was a Rollin' Stone*

Quiz 5

1. a. George Harrison, with his *Wonderwall Music* album, released in the U.K. on November 1, 1968 . . . John Lennon was the first ex-Beatle to release a solo single
2. c. Jeff Beck, whom he had worked with the prior year
3. b. David Bowie, whose first U.S. hit *Space Oddity* had also just reached the Top 40
4. b. *Hello It's Me,* Rundgren's solo version peaking at #5 in December, 1973
5. a. Sweet Sensation, who were from England
6. b. Capricorn
7. a. *Take it Easy*
8. a. Abba
9. b. Bobbie Gentry
10. c. Grunt

****

Questions 11-16: SONG HITS

11. b. *Cracklin' Rosie,* in 1970
12. a. *Take Me Home, Country Roads*
13. a. *The Wreck of the Edmund Fitzgerald*
14. c. *Whole Lotta Love,* in 1969
15. c. *Someday Never Comes,* in 1972
16. b. *Black Water* . . . although released earlier, *Long Train Runnin'* did not reach #1

****

Questions 17-20: HARDER QUESTIONS

17. b. Rufus . . . American Breed's Kevin Murphy was a founding member of Rufus
18. a. *Midnight Plane to Houston*
19. c. A Group With No Name
20. c. *Papa Was a Rollin' Stone* . . . the original song was so long — 11:45 — that the 'B' side of the single consisted solely of the instrumental portion . . . amazingly, it won the Grammy award as an instrumental !

Quiz 6

1. Which of the following singers was NOT Jamaican ?

        a. Carl Douglas

        b. Johnny Nash

        c. Jimmy Cliff

****

2. In what year did Kenny Rogers release his first single ?

        a. 1958

        b. 1964

        c. 1968

****

3. In Elton John's #1 autobiographical album *Captain Fantastic and the Brown Dirt Cowboy*, Elton John was portrayed as "Captain Fantastic". Who was the "Brown Dirt Cowboy" ?

        a. David Bowie

        b. Bernie Taupin

        c. Nigel Olsson

****

4. What event in *Alone Again (Naturally)* had strong personal significance in Gilbert O'Sullivan's life ?

        a. the death of his father

        b. his marriage disappointment

        c. neither

5. What Electric Light Orchestra song was a remake of a minor hit by their earlier incarnation, the Move ?

      a. *Do Ya*

      b. *Telephone Line*

      c. *Don't Bring Me Down*

****

6. In what iconic movie did *I Can See Clearly Now* singer Johnny Nash have a major part ?

      a. *Guess Who's Coming to Dinner*

      b. *The Blackboard Jungle*

      c. *Take a Giant Step*

****

7. Which of the following singers was NOT part of Dionne Warwick & Friends' #1 hit *That's What Friends Are For* ?

      a. Roberta Flack

      b. Elton John

      c. Stevie Wonder

****

8. On the soundtrack for which movie did David Carradine's 1976 hit *I'm Easy* appear ?

      a. *Silver Bears*

      b. *Nasty Habits*

      c. *Nashville*

9. What performer's real (birth) first/middle names are Rigdon Osmond ?

       a. Little Jimmy Osmond

       b. Rick Dees

       c. Donny Osmond

****

10. On which label did David Bowie record his earlier hits, including *Fame* ?

       a. RCA

       b. EMI–America

       c. Polydor

****

Questions 11-16: SONG HITS

11. According to Billboard's Hot 100 singles chart, what was the #1 song for 1974 ?

       a. *The Way We Were*

       b. *Seasons In the Sun*

       c. *Bennie and the Jets*

****

12. What was Aerosmith's first single to break into the Top 40 ?

       a. *Last Child*

       b. *Sweet Emotion*

       c. *Dream On*

13. What was Isaac Hayes' only U.S. #1 hit ?

    a. *Walk On By*

    b. *Don't Let Go*

    c. *Theme From Shaft*

****

14. What was Peaches & Herb's first U.S. Billboard Top 40 hit ?

    a. *Shake Your Groove Thing*

    b. *Close Your Eyes*

    c. *Let's Fall In Love*

****

15. Which of the following hits charted highest for Earth, Wind & Fire on the U.S. Billboard singles chart ?

    a. *After the Love Has Gone*

    b. *Shining Star*

    c. *Sing a Song*

****

16. What was Cat Stevens' last U.S. Top 20 hit ?

    a. *Oh Very Young*

    b. *Another Saturday Night*

    c. *Where Do the Children Play ?*

17. What underground psychedelic '60s band did
ZZ Top leader Billy Gibbons form ?

      a. Moby Grape

      b. the Moving Sidewalks

      c. Southwest F.O.B.

****

18. What was the title of the demo-single of the song
later recorded by Johnnie Taylor as *Disco Lady*?

      a. *Disco Crazy*

      b. *Let's Go Crazy*

      c. *Disco Baby*

****

19. Which of the following was NOT a nickname at
one time for singer Rod Stewart ?

      a. "the red-haired bandit"

      b. "the Tartan terror"

      c. "rooster-top"

****

20. Which group is being referred to with the
comment that their "audience wasn't the sensitive
crowd. It was the guy who just dropped three
downs, swigged a bottle of Boone's Farm, and did
a lot of hanging out".

      a. Supertramp

      b. the Steve Miller Band

      c. Grand Funk Railroad

Quiz 6

1. b. Johnny Nash, who was born in the U.S.
2. a. 1958, on the *Carlton* label, listed as Kenneth Rogers
3. b. Bernie Taupin
4. c. neither . . . "None of the situations in the song ever happened to me," he later admitted
5. a. *Do Ya,* which reached #24 in 1977 — the Move's version was released in 1972
6. c. *Take a Giant Step,* the 1958 movie similar to and as memorable as 1967's *Guess Who's Coming to Dinner*
7. a. Roberta Flack . . . Gladys Knight was the other female part of "Friends" along with Dionne
8. c. *Nashville*
9. b. Rick Dees, born Rigdon Osmond Dees III . . . his *Disco Duck* topped the charts in 1976
10. a. RCA

```
************************************************************
```

Questions 11-16: SONG HITS

11. a. *The Way We Were,* by Barbra Streisand
12. b. *Sweet Emotion,* in 1975
13. c. *Theme From Shaft*
14. c. *Let's Fall In Love,* in 1967
15. b. *Shining Star,* #1 in 1975
16. b. *Another Saturday Night*

```
************************************************************
```

Questions 17-20: HARDER QUESTIONS

17. b. the Moving Sidewalks, who opened for the Jimi Hendrix Experience in a 1968 concert
18. c. *Disco Baby*
19. a. "the red-haired bandit"
20. c. Grand Funk Railroad

Quiz 7

1. Which label did Led Zeppelin form in 1974 ?

   a. Big Tree

   b. Swan Song

   c. Casablanca

****

2. What religious affiliation included '70s rock stars Seals & Crofts ?

   a. Jehovah's Witness

   b. Christian Science

   c. Baha'i Faith

****

3. On which song did Beach Boys members Carl Wilson and Bruce Johnston contribute backing vocals ?

   a. *We're An American Band*

   b. *Don't Let the Sun Go Down On Me*

   c. *Mandy*

****

4. Who first recorded the 1974 Three Dog Night hit *The Show Must Go On* ?

   a. Leo Sayer

   b. Gilbert O'Sullivan

   c. Paper Lace

5. Who earned the nickname "the Space Cowboy" ?

      a. Glen Campbell

      b. David Bowie

      c. Steve Miller

****

6. Mick Taylor replaced Brian Jones as a member of the Rolling Stones. Who later replaced Mick Taylor ?

      a. Tara Richard

      b. Dave Mason

      c. Ron Wood

****

7. What top British band of the late '60s was Rod Stewart NOT a member of ?

      a. the Hollies

      b. the Faces

      c. the Jeff Beck Group

****

8. What was the real (birth) name of Janis Ian ?

      a. Janice O'Malley

      b. Janis Fink

      c. Janet Moore

9. On which label did Jefferson Starship record their hits, including *Miracles* ?

        a. Grunt

        b. Harvest

        c. Kirshner

****

10. Which group featured members including Steve, Tom, Joey and Brad ?

        a. Bad Company

        b. Aerosmith

        c. Earth, Wind & Fire

****

Questions 11-16: SONG HITS

11. What was the O'Jays' first U.S. Billboard Top 40 hit ?

        a. *Back Stabbers*

        b. *Love Train*

        c. *Put Your Hands Together*

****

12. What was Fleetwood Mac's first single to reach the U.S. Billboard Top 20 record charts ?

        a. *Say You Love Me*

        b. *Rhiannon (Will You Ever Win)*

        c. *Don't Stop*

13. Which of the following hits charted highest for War on the U.S. Billboard singles chart ?

   a. *The Cisco Kid*

   b. *Why Can't We Be Friends?*

   c. *Low Rider*

****

14. What was Jimmy Buffett's first U.S. Billboard Top 40 hit ?

   a. *Cheeseburger in Paradise*

   b. *Come Monday*

   c. *Margaritaville*

****

15. What was Simon & Garfunkel's last U.S. Top 20 hit ?

   a. *My Little Town*

   b. *El Condor Pasa*

   c. *Cecilia*

****

16. What was Eric Clapton's only #1 hit in the '70s and '80s ?

   a. *Lay Down Sally*

   b. *Layla*

   c. *I Shot the Sheriff*

17. What group did David Bowie sing for after he first changed his name from David Jones ?

      a. the Mannish Boys

      b. Feathers

      c. the Hype

****

18. A hit for the Four Seasons in 1975, what was the originally intended subject of the song later titled *December '63 (Oh What a Night)* ?

      a. it was about a wedding night

      b. it was about a rival gang confrontation

      c. it was about prohibition

****

19. Which 1976 song was featured in a Kodak television commercial ?

      a. *Sara Smile*

      b. *Strange Magic*

      c. *Times of Your Life*

****

20. Who was *Billboard Magazine* referring to when they said that he "could have a big following when he finds his own style" ?

      a. Bob Seger

      b. Bob Dylan

      c. Bruce Springsteen

answers
Quiz 7

1. b. Swan Song
2. c. Baha'i Faith
3. b. *Don't Let the Sun Go Down On Me,* the 1974 Elton John hit
4. a. Leo Sayer, whose version was released earlier in the year
5. c. Steve Miller
6. c. Ron Wood, who replaced Taylor in 1975
7. a. the Hollies
8. b. Janis Fink
9. a. Grunt
10. b. Aerosmith

****

Questions 11-16: SONG HITS

11. a. *Back Stabbers*
12. b. *Rhiannon (Will You Ever Win),* in May, 1976
13. a. *The Cisco Kid,* reaching #2 for 2 weeks in 1973 . . . Eric Burdon & War reached #3 with *Spill the Wine* in 1970
14. b. *Come Monday*
15. a. *My Little Town,* in 1975
16. c. *I Shot the Sheriff,* #1 in 1974, a song written by Bob Marley

****

Questions 17-20: HARDER QUESTIONS

17. a. the Mannish Boys, named after a Muddy Waters song
18. c. it was about the prohibition of alcohol in the 1920s
19. c. *Times of Your Life,* Paul Anka's hit
20. b. Bob Dylan

Quiz 8

1. What recreational activity was Ted Nugent well-known for ?
   - a. hunting
   - b. hang-gliding
   - c. mountain climbing

****

2. What was the actual incident that later inspired Elton John's *Someone Saved My Life Tonight* ?
   - a. a reunion between Elton John and Bernie Taupin
   - b. the winning of three Grammy awards
   - c. a suicide attempt by Elton John

****

3. What group was led by Lonesome Dave Peverett ?
   - a. Pilot
   - b. Foghat
   - c. Free

****

4. Who wrote Joe Cocker's 1975 hit *You Are So Beautiful* ?
   - a. Billy Joel
   - b. Jackson Browne
   - c. Billy Preston

5. How did the Swedish rock group Abba get their name ?

    a. from a Swedish word meaning "favorite"

    b. from the first letters of the members' names

    c. from the first name listed in a Swedish telephone book

****

6. *Billy, Don't Be a Hero* was a tale written about which war ?

    a. the Civil War

    b. World War II

    c. Viet Nam

****

7. Who had the lead role in the movie *Tommy* ?

    a. Elton John

    b. Roger Daltry

    c. David Bowie

****

8. Brian Connolly was lead singer for which group ?

    a. Wet Willie

    b. Starbuck

    c. Sweet

9. Which group featured members including Les, Stuart and Eric ?

        a. 10cc

        b. Electric Light Orchestra

        c. the Bay City Rollers

****

10. What was Alice Cooper's real (birth) name ?

        a. Reginald Dwight

        b. Vincent Furnier

        c. Arnold Wiggins

****

Questions 11-16: SONG HITS

11. What was Pablo Cruise's first U.S. Billboard Top 40 hit ?

        a. *Love Will Find a Way*

        b. *Cool Love*

        c. *Whatcha Gonna Do?*

****

12. What was Seals & Crofts' last U.S. Top 40 hit ?

        a. *Get Closer*

        b. *You're the Love*

        c. *I'll Play For You*

13. Which of the following hits charted highest for the O'Jays on the U.S. Billboard singles chart ?

a. *Back Stabbers*

b. *Used Ta Be My Girl*

c. *Love Train*

****

14. What was Natalie Cole's first U.S. Billboard Top 40 hit ?

a. *Our Love*

b. *This Will Be*

c. *Inseparable*

****

15. What was Rod Stewart's first U.S. #1 hit ?

a. *Maggie May*

b. *Da Ya Think I'm Sexy ?*

c. *Tonight's the Night (Gonna Be Alright)*

****

16. What was Billy Ocean's first U.S. Billboard Top 40 hit ?

a. *Caribbean Queen*

b. *Loverboy*

c. *Love Really Hurts Without You*

17. As a young girl, Olivia Newton-John won a contest for being what ?

    a. a Hayley Mills look-alike

    b. the best chess player in the city

    c. the most talented girl in her high school

****

18. What was a former name for Grand Funk Railroad ?

    a. Terry Knight & the Pack

    b. Mark's Mascots

    c. the Grey Hounds

****

19. For which of the following companies did Barry Manilow write television jingles ?

    a. McDonald's

    b. State Farm Insurance

    c. Pepsi

****

20. What other group did two members of Hamilton, Joe Frank & Reynolds form in the mid-'70s ?

    a. Hamilton, Joe Frank & Dennison

    b. Humble Pie

    c. the Chesapeakes

answers

Quiz 8

1. a. hunting
2. c. a suicide attempt by Elton John, brought on by second thoughts and ensuing depression regarding a forthcoming marriage ... The marriage plans were terminated, the song became a testimonial and a hit, and Elton John and his music lives on
3. b. Foghat
4. c. Billy Preston
5. b. from the first letters of the members' names: Agnetha — Bjorn — Benny — Anni-Frida
6. a. the Civil War
7. b. Roger Daltry
8. c. Sweet
9. c. the Bay City Rollers
10. b. Vincent Damon Furnier

****

Questions 11-16: SONG HITS

11. c. *Whatcha Gonna Do?*
12. b. *You're the Love*
13. c. *Love Train,* #1 in 1973
14. b. *This Will Be*
15. a. *Maggie May*
16. c. *Love Really Hurts Without You,* in 1976

****

Questions 17-20: HARDER QUESTIONS

17. a. a Hayley Mills look-alike, at age twelve — she won a trip to London, which sparked her music career
18. a. Terry Knight & the Pack
19. b. State Farm Insurance, though he did sing on McDonald's, Pepsi, and Jack-in-the-Box commercials, among others
20. a. Hamilton, Joe Frank & Dennison (the duo together with Alan Dennison)

Quiz 9

1. How did the members of Kiss first meet ?
   - a. by responding to a newspaper ad
   - b. in a musical play dress rehearsal
   - c. in a kissing contest

****

2. Who did the group Edward Bear name themselves after ?
   - a. Winnie the Pooh
   - b. a legendary Indian chief
   - c. two British blues singers

****

3. What country are the Bay City Rollers from ?
   - a. Scotland
   - b. Canada
   - c. Ireland

****

4. Who was Henry Gross, whose single *Shannon* reached #6 in 1976, the original lead guitarist for ?
   - a. Sha-Na-Na
   - b. Edward Bear
   - c. Rufus

5. What incident left *Superfly* singer Curtis Mayfield paralyzed ?

      a. a fall from his roof

      b. a stage mishap

      c. a train derailment

****

6. With which of the following did Paul McCartney NOT sing in a duet hit single ?

      a. Michael Jackson

      b. Stevie Wonder

      c. Ray Charles

****

7. Major Harris, whose single *Love Won't Let Me Wait* was a Top 5 single in 1975, had been a member of what early '70s group ?

      a. the Stylistics

      b. the Chi-Lites

      c. the Delfonics

****

8. Who won the Grammy for Best New Artist of the Year for 1976 ?

      a. Heart

      b. the Starland Vocal Band

      c. George Benson

9. Which group featured members including Captain Cold, Duke, Powerpack and Hammer ?

      a. Rose Royce

      b. Earth, Wind & Fire

      c. Heatwave

****

10. In what movie did Aerosmith appear, portraying villains ?

      a. *Jesus Christ Superstar*

      b. *Sgt. Pepper's Lonely Hearts Club Band*

      c. *Tommy*

****

Questions 11-16: SONG HITS

11. *(I Can't Get No) Satisfaction* was the Rolling Stones' first #1 hit. What was their last ?

      a. *Miss You*

      b. *Start Me Up*

      c. *Honky Tony Women*

****

12. What was Jermaine Jackson's first U.S. Billboard Top 40 hit ?

      a. *Let's Get Serious*

      b. *Daddy's Home*

      c. *Dynamite*

13. What was Carly Simon's last solo U.S. Top 40 hit ?

      a. *You Belong to Me*

      b. *Jesse*

      c. *Nobody Does It Better*

****

14. Which of the following hits charted highest for the Stylistics on the U.S. Billboard singles chart ?

      a. *You Make Me Feel Brand New*

      b. *You Are Everything*

      c. *Betcha By Golly, Wow*

****

15. What was the Bay City Rollers' only U.S. #1 hit ?

      a. *Money Honey*

      b. *Saturday Night*

      c. *You Made Me Believe In Magic*

****

16. Which of the following hits charted highest for the Commodores on the U.S. Billboard singles chart ?

      a. *Brick House*

      b. *Still*

      c. *Three Times a Lady*

17. What commercially-unsuccessful '70s group did former Box Tops leader Alex Chilton form ?

        a. the Fugs

        b. Hotlegs

        c. Big Star

****

18. Which rock star was born with two different eye colors, one blue and one grey ?

        a. David Essex

        b. Billy Idol

        c. David Bowie

****

19. After what were Patti Labelle & the Blue-Belles named ?

        a. a toy train manufacturer

        b. a record label

        c. a bread company

****

20. What inspired Elton John to write *Philadelphia Freedom* with Bernie Taupin ?

        a. a political demonstration

        b. a picnic

        c. a tennis team

answers

Quiz 9

1. a. by responding to a newspaper ad
2. a. Winnie the Pooh, whose "real" name is Edward Bear
3. a. Scotland
4. a. Sha–Na–Na
5. b. a stage mishap . . . in heavy winds, a lighting rig fell on him during an outdoor concert in 1990
6. c. Ray Charles
7. c. the Delfonics
8. b. the Starland Vocal Band
9. a. Rose Royce
10. b. *Sgt. Pepper's Lonely Hearts Club Band*

****

Questions 11-16: SONG HITS

11. a. *Miss You*, in 1978
12. b. *Daddy's Home*, in 1973
13. b. *Jesse*, in 1980
14. a. *You Make Me Feel Brand New*, reaching #2 in 1974
15. b. *Saturday Night*
16. c. *Three Times a Lady*, #1 for 2 weeks in 1978

****

Questions 17-20: HARDER QUESTIONS

17. c. Big Star
18. c. David Bowie, an eye–color–mismatch "oddity" that approximately one person in 12,000 is born with
19. b. a record label, Bluebelle Records, a subsidiary label of the company they recorded with
20. c. the Philadelphia Freedoms tennis team, a team Elton followed with great enthusiasm

Quiz 10

1. What was the name of Bob Seger's band during the time of *Ramblin' Gamblin' Man*?

      a. Bob Seger & the Last Heard
      b. the Bob Seger System
      c. the Quaker City Boys

****

2. What late '70s group was *Ghostbusters* singer Ray Parker, Jr. the lead singer for?

      a. Heatwave
      b. L.T.D
      c. Raydio

****

3. In which album did Kiss first appear without the now-famous Kiss makeup?

      a. *Kiss*
      b. *Kiss Unmasked*
      c. *Lick It Up*

****

4. *Go Away Little Girl* and *The Loco-Motion* were the first cover versions of a previous #1 song of the '60s to also reach #1 in the U.S. singles chart in the '70s. What was the third song to accomplish this feat?

      a. *Please Mr. Postman*
      b. *Our Day Will Come*
      c. *When Will I Be Loved*

5. According to the Billboard Hot 100 singles chart, what was the most successful song for Arista Records during the '70s & '80s ?

        a. *Ghost Busters*

        b. *Every Woman In the World*

        c. *That's What Friends Are For*

****

6. Which '70s band was formed from an ad placed in the local newspaper, seeking singers with mustaches who could also dance ?

        a. the Village People

        b. the Commodores

        c. Queen

****

7. Who was dubbed as having a sensual "pillow talk" vocal style ?

        a. Rod Stewart

        b. Barry White

        c. Billy Paul

****

8. Who wrote Rufus' 1974 hit *Tell Me Something Good*, written specially for female lead singer Chaka Khan ?

        a. James Brown

        b. Sylvester "Sly" Stone

        c. Stevie Wonder

9. Mark Farner was lead singer of what '70s group ?

      a. Deep Purple

      b. Grand Funk

      c. Guess Who

****

10. In what movie did Jigsaw's 1975 hit *Sky High* appear ?

      a. *Nashville*

      b. *The Towering Inferno*

      c. *The Dragon Flies*

****

Questions 11-16: SONG HITS

11. What was Lynyrd Skynyrd's first U.S. Billboard Top 40 hit ?

      a. *Sweet Home Alabama*

      b. *What's Your Name*

      c. *Free Bird*

****

12. What was the Bay City Rollers' last U.S. Top 40 hit ?

      a. *The Way I Feel Tonight*

      b. *You Made Me Believe In Magic*

      c. *I Only Want to Be With You*

13. What was George Benson's first U.S. Billboard Top 40 hit ?

   a. *The Greatest Love Of All*
   b. *This Masquerade*
   c. *On Broadway*

****

14. Which of the following hits charted highest for Kenny Rogers on the U.S. Billboard singles chart ?

   a. *Lady*
   b. *She Believes In Me*
   c. *Lucille*

****

15. What was Seals & Crofts' first U.S. Billboard Top 40 hit ?

   a. *Diamond Girl*
   b. *Summer Breeze*
   c. *Get Closer*

****

16. What was the Four Seasons' last U.S. Top 20 hit ?

   a. *Who Loves You*
   b. *December, 1963 (Oh, What a Night)*
   c. *Will You Love Me Tomorrow*

17. Which of the following artists had a #1 hit in the U.S. and in England, but then never again charted in either country ?

> a. Toby Beau
>
> b. Bob Welch
>
> c. the Floaters

****

18. Styx was originally known as TW4. Why did they use this abbreviation rather than the name the initials stood for ?

> a. to avoid confusion with the group the Trade Winds
>
> b. to satisfy angry Trans World Airlines lawyers
>
> c. to capitalize on the British success of the DC5

****

19. What was a former name for the band Kiss ?

> a. the Cramp Stompers
>
> b. Bullfrog Bheer
>
> c. Cheshire Cat

****

20. What song did Electric Light Orchestra leader Jeff Lynne reportedly say inspired him to form the band ?

> a. *Crimson & Clover* (Tommy James & the Shondells)
>
> b. *Journey to the Center of the Mind* (Amboy Dukes)
>
> c. *I Am the Walrus* (Beatles)

Quiz 10

1. b. the Bob Seger System
2. c. Raydio
3. c. *Lick It Up*
4. a. *Please Mr. Postman* . . . the Marvelettes did it in 1961, the Carpenters did it in 1975
5. c. *That's What Friends Are For,* by Dionne & Friends
6. a. the Village People
7. b. Barry White
8. c. Stevie Wonder
9. b. Grand Funk
10. c. *The Dragon Flies*

****

Questions 11-16: SONG HITS

11. a. *Sweet Home Alabama*
12. a. *The Way I Feel Tonight*
13. b. *This Masquerade*
14. a. *Lady,* #1 for 6 weeks in 1980
15. b. *Summer Breeze*
16. b. *December, 1963 (Oh, What a Night),* in 1976

****

Questions 17-20: HARDER QUESTIONS

17. c. the Floaters, with their 1977 hit *Float On*
18. a. to avoid confusion with the group the Trade Winds . . . the Styx members were originally called the Tradewinds when they formed in 1964, but with the 1965 hit *New York's a Lonely Town* by the New York group Trade Winds, they elected to avoid any possible future confusion
19. b. Bullfrog Bheer
20. c. *I Am the Walrus* (Beatles)

Quiz 11

1. What was the name of the 1979 television documentary film on the Who ?
   - a. *Tommy*
   - b. *Quadrophenia*
   - c. *The Kids are Alright*

****

2. Who wrote Carly Simon's 1978 hit *You Belong to Me* ?
   - a. Carole King
   - b. James Taylor
   - c. Michael McDonald

****

3. Why did Kansas change their name from White Clover ?
   - a. they wanted a name that avoided racial association
   - b. another local group was already called White Clover
   - c. the band members were all from Kansas

****

4. In what TV soap opera did Rick Springfield have a regular role ?
   - a. *As The World Turns*
   - b. *The Guiding Light*
   - c. *General Hospital*

5. According to the Billboard Hot 100 singles chart, what was the most successful song for Elektra Records during the '70s & '80s ?

      a. *Another One Bites the Dust*

      b. *You're So Vain*

      c. *Steal Away*

****

6. Singer Boz Scaggs was an original member of what '70s group ?

      a. Foreigner

      b. the Steve Miller Band

      c. Bob Seger's Silver Bullet Band

****

7. Who contributed background vocals on David Bowie's 1975 hit *Fame* ?

      a. John Lennon

      b. Freddie Mercury

      c. Mick Jagger

****

8. Who was NOT a member of the group Toby Beau ?

      a. Toby Beau

      b. Balde Silva

      c. Danny McKenna

9. What was Meat Loaf's real (birth) name ?

      a. Jonathan Joseph Spiers

      b. Samuel Hammersmith

      c. Marvin Lee Aday

****

10. On which label did the Commodores record their hits, including *Three Times a Lady*?

      a. Motown

      b. Cotillion

      c. Warner Brothers

****

Questions 11-16: SONG HITS

11. What was Ambrosia's first U.S. Billboard Top 40 hit ?

      a. *How Much I Feel*

      b. *Holdin' On To Yesterday*

      c. *Biggest Part of Me*

****

12. What was Leo Sayer's last U.S. Top 20 hit ?

      a. *When I Need You*

      b. *More Than I Can Say*

      c. *You Make Me Feel Like Dancing*

13. What was Foreigner's first single to reach the U.S. Billboard Top 20 record charts ?

    a. *Cold As Ice*

    b. *Feels Like the First Time*

    c. *Hot Blooded*

****

14. Which of the following hits charted highest for Linda Ronstadt on the U.S. Billboard singles chart ?

    a. *You're No Good*

    b. *Blue Bayou*

    c. *When Will I Be Loved*

****

15. Which of the following #1 hits charted the longest for Diana Ross on the U.S. Billboard singles chart ?

    a. *Love Hangover*

    b. *Upside Down*

    c. *Ain't No Mountain High Enough*

****

16. What was Kiss's last U.S. Top 40 hit ?

    a. *Calling Dr. Love*

    b. *Christine Sixteen*

    c. *I Was Made For Lovin' You*

HARDER QUESTIONS (17-20): 2 points each
(4 points if you can answer the question without the three choices !)

17. What was the title of a 1977 disco song including the *I Love Lucy* theme song ?

   a. *Disco Lucy*

   b. *Get Dancin'*

   c. *Disco Lady*

****

18. What name did the pre-Commodores use while performing together in college ?

   a. the Collegians

   b. the Crimson Tide

   c. the Mighty Mystics

****

19. Which rock group appeared on Paul Lynde's televised 1975 Halloween Special ?

   a. Queen

   b. Kiss

   c. Fleetwood Mac

****

20. Who was referred to in the following critical review, being called "a prototype late-'70s rock phenomenon: a rocker who honed his craft in the '60s and bided his time until the market was right for his well-produced encyclopedia of riffs."

   a. Steve Miller

   b. Bruce Springsteen

   c. Bob Seger

Quiz 11

1. c. *The Kids are Alright*
2. c. Michael McDonald
3. c. the band members were all from Kansas
4. c. *General Hospital*, in which he played Noah Drake
5. a. *Another One Bites the Dust*, by Queen
6. b. the Steve Miller Band
7. a. John Lennon
8. a. Toby Beau, which was actually the name of a wooden shrimp boat
9. c. Marvin Lee Aday
10. a. Motown

****

Questions 11-16: SONG HITS

11. b. *Holdin' On To Yesterday*, in 1975
12. b. *More Than I Can Say*
13. b. *Feels Like the First Time*, in May, 1977
14. a. *You're No Good*, #1 in 1975
15. b. *Upside Down*, #1 for 4 weeks in 1980
16. c. *I Was Made For Lovin' You*

****

Questions 17-20: HARDER QUESTIONS

17. a. *Disco Lucy*, by the Wilton Play Street Band
18. c. the Mighty Mystics . . . they then merged with the Jays, but the name too closely resembled the O'Jays — the name "Commodores" was eventually picked at random from the dictionary
19. b. Kiss
20. a. Steve Miller

Quiz 12

1. In which country did Cheap Trick's 1978 concert sell out within two hours ?

    a. England

    b. Japan

    c. Australia

****

2. With what famous blues band did three of the original members of Fleetwood Mac play ?

    a. John Mayall's Bluesbreakers

    b. the Blues Magoos

    c. the Blues Project

****

3. Which singer scored his first solo Top 40 U.S. hit the most years after his group first scored its first Billboard hit ?

    a. Smokey Robinson

    b. Mick Jagger

    c. Barry Gibb

****

4. *TSOP* by MFSB was the theme song for which '70s show ?

    a. *Night Flight*

    b. *Soul Train*

    c. *The Midnight Special*

5. Barry DeVorzon's 1976 hit *Nadia's Theme* was featured in the television soap opera *The Young and the Restless.* But what was the song originally entitled ?

      a. *Bound for Glory*

      b. *Jack's First Night Out*

      c. *Cotton's Dream*

****

6. What unique rock and roll production did each of the four members of Kiss participate in during 1978 ?

  a. each hosted their own rock-radio talk show in different cities

  b. each sponsored a different commercial product on TV

  c. each released a solo album

****

7. Members of what group backed up Bob Welch on his 1978 hit *Sentimental Lady* ?

      a. Atlanta Rhythm Section

      b. Fleetwood Mac

      c. Boston

****

8. In what movie did the Bee Gees hit *Stayin' Alive* appear ?

      a. *Saturday Night Fever*

      b. *American Graffiti*

      c. *Grease*

9. What group included members named Peter, John, Ronn and Wayne ?

        a. Styx

        b. Sweet

        c. Player

****

10. On which label did the Electric Light Orchestra NOT record their earliest hits, including *Evil Woman* and *Turn to Stone* ?

        a. UA

        b. Jet

        c. Chelsea

****

Questions 11-16: SONG HITS

11. What was David Bowie's first U.S. Billboard Top 40 hit ?

        a. *Space Oddity*

        b. *Fame*

        c. *China Girl*

****

12. What was the Bee Gees' last U.S. Top 20 hit ?

        a. *Love You Inside Out*

        b. *Tragedy*

        c. *Too Much Heaven*

13. Which of the following hits charted highest for Anne Murray on the U.S. Billboard singles chart ?

   a. *You Needed Me*

   b. *Danny's Song*

   c. *Snowbird*

****

14. What was Abba's first single to reach the U.S. Billboard Top 20 record charts ?

   a. *Waterloo*

   b. *Dancing Queen*

   c. *Fernando*

****

15. What was the O'Jays' last U.S. Top 40 hit ?

   a. *I Love Music*

   b. *Used Ta Be My Girl*

   c. *Forever Mine*

****

16. What was Peter Frampton's first U.S. Billboard Top 40 hit ?

   a. *Baby, I Love Your Way*

   b. *Show Me the Way*

   c. *I'm In You*

HARDER QUESTIONS (17-20): 2 points each
(4 points if you can answer the question without the three choices !)

17. While in high school, Steve Miller formed his first band, the Marksmen Combo, which included another future star who, in fact, learned the guitar from Steve Miller. Who was this friend ?

    a. Eddie Van Halen

    b. Richie Sambora

    c. Boz Scaggs

****

18. Which of the following was NOT a name that Kool & the Gang once called themselves ?

    a. the Rivieras

    b. the Jazziacs

    c. the New Dimensions

****

19. What song caused Billy Joel to be banned by Catholic radio stations due to supposedly heretical lyrics ?

    a. *Honesty*

    b. *Only the Good Die Young*

    c. *Keeping the Faith*

****

20. From what did the British band Supertramp get its name ?

    a. a dredging rig

    b. a book

    c. the movies *Superman* and *Lady & the Tramp*

a n s w e r s
Quiz 12

1. b. Japan
2. a. John Mayall's Bluesbreakers
3. b. Mick Jagger, whose 1985 hit, *Just Another Night,* came 21 years after the Rolling Stones' first Billboard hit, *Not Fade Away*
4. b. *Soul Train*
5. c. *Cotton's Dream,* from the 1971 movie *Bless the Beasts and Children*
6. c. dressed up in "Kiss" attire, each released a solo album
7. b. Fleetwood Mac . . . specifically, Christine McVie and Lindsey Buckingham . . . Bob Welch had been a member of Fleetwood Mac in the group's early days . . .
8. a. *Saturday Night Fever*
9. c. Player
10. c. Chelsea

****

Questions 11-16: SONG HITS

11. a. *Space Oddity*
12. a. *Love You Inside Out,* in 1979
13. a. *You Needed Me,* #1 in 1978
14. a. *Waterloo,* in 1974
15. c. *Forever Mine,* in 1980
16. b. *Show Me the Way*

****

Questions 17-20: HARDER QUESTIONS

17. c. Boz Scaggs
18. a. the Rivieras
19. b. *Only the Good Die Young*
20. b. the 1910 book *The Autobiography of a Supertramp,* by W. H. Davies

Quiz 13

1. Who was Elton John's *Empty Garden* written about ?
   > a. Marilyn Monroe
   > b. John F. Kennedy
   > c. John Lennon

****

2. What band did members of the 1979 group the Buggles join in 1980 ?
   > a. Styx
   > b. Blondie
   > c. Yes

****

3. Comparing the British and U.S. Billboard charts, which of the following songs reached #1 in one country but did not crack the Top 20 in the other country ?
   > a. *Mull of Kintyre* / Paul McCartney
   > b. *It's a Heartache* / Bonnie Tyler
   > c. *How Deep Is Your Love* / Bee Gees

****

4. Two of the following music stars were at one time in their career afraid of flying — which of the following was NOT ever afraid to fly ?
   > a. David Bowie
   > b. Aretha Franklin
   > c. Bruce Springsteen

5. According to the Billboard Hot 100 singles chart, what was the most successful song for Atlantic Records during the '70s & '80s ?

　　　a. *Waiting For a Girl Like You*
　　　b. *Le Freak*
　　　c. *First Time Ever I Saw Your Face*

✳✳✳

6. How many changes did the Jefferson Airplane / Starship have in their band's lineup over the years ?

　　　a. 12
　　　b. 24
　　　c. 33

✳✳✳

7. What band was Joan Jett a member of in the '70s ?

　　　a. the Runaways
　　　b. Heart
　　　c. .38 Special

✳✳✳

8. In what movie did Barry Manilow's 1978 hit *Copacabana (At the Copa)* appear ?

　　　a. *Midnight Express*
　　　b. *Foul Play*
　　　c. *Boulevard Nights*

9. On which label did the Steve Miller Band record their hits, including *Fly Like An Eagle* ?

        a. Asylum

        b. Capitol

        c. ABC

****

10. What group was led by members named Buck Dharma and Eric Bloom ?

        a. Kansas

        b. Exile

        c. Blue Öyster Cult

****

Questions 11-16: SONG HITS

11. What was Donna Summer's first #1 hit ?

        a. *MacArthur Park*

        b. *Last Dance*

        c. *Hot Stuff*

****

12. What was Styx's first single to reach the U.S. Billboard Top 20 record charts ?

        a. *Babe*

        b. *Lady*

        c. *Come Sail Away*

13. Which of the following hits charted highest for John Lennon on the U.S. Billboard singles chart ?

    a. *Imagine*

    b. *(Just Like) Starting Over*

    c. *Whatever Gets You Thru the Night*

****

14. What was Fleetwood Mac's only #1 U.S. hit ?

    a. *Dreams*

    b. *Go Your Own Way*

    c. *Hold Me*

****

15. What was Boz Scaggs' first U.S. Billboard Top 20 hit ?

    a. *Lowdown*

    b. *Lido Shuffle*

    c. *Miss Sun*

****

16. What was Eddie Money's first U.S. Billboard Top 40 hit ?

    a. *Baby Hold On*

    b. *Take Me Home Tonight*

    c. *Two Tickets To Paradise*

17. What was a former name for the band Queen ?

   a. the Smile

   b. the Mercuries

   c. the Wreck

****

18. Johnny Mathis' song *Wonderful! Wonderful!* spent 39 weeks on the U.S. singles Hot 100 in 1957. What song from 1978 topped that mark, staying on the charts for 40 weeks ?

   a. *Night Fever*

   b. *Le Freak*

   c. *I Go Crazy*

****

19. What event resulted in the Police having a new image as Punk Rockers in the late '70s ?

   a. an appearance at a disco lounge

   b. a confrontational interview

   c. a television ad

****

20. What inspired the Bee Gees' song, *Jive Talkin'* ?

   a. a gangster movie

   b. an elevator ride

   c. railroad tracks

Quiz 13

1. c. John Lennon, as a tribute
2. c. Yes
3. a. *Mull of Kintyre* / Paul McCartney . . . #1 in England, but only reaching #33 in the U.S.
4. c. Bruce Springsteen
5. b. *Le Freak,* the hit by Chic which sold over 4 million copies
6. c. 33, including returning members
7. a. the Runaways, from 1975–1978
8. b. *Foul Play*
9. b. Capitol
10. c. Blue Öyster Cult

****

Questions 11-16: SONG HITS

11. a. *MacArthur Park,* in 1978
12. b. *Lady,* in 1975
13. b. *(Just Like) Starting Over,* #1 for 5 weeks in 1980
14. a. *Dreams,* #1 for one week in 1977
15. a. *Lowdown*
16. a. *Baby Hold On*

****

Questions 17-20: HARDER QUESTIONS

17. a. the Smile
18. c. *I Go Crazy,* by Paul Davis . . . unusually enough, neither reached #1 . . . Mathis' song reached only as high as #14, and Davis' song managed to climb to #7
19. c. a television ad (in 1978, the Police appeared in a Wrigley's Chewing Gum television ad, in which they had their hair dyed blond . . . their image quickly turned to Punk Rockers, an image they maintained for a couple of years)
20. c. railroad tracks . . . on a nightly drive home with his wife, Barry Gibb would often cross train tracks . . . one day, his wife commented on the "chunka–chunka" sound, adding "it's our *'drive talking'*" . . . Bingo ! Sometimes it happens just that easily !

Quiz 14

1. From what country did Blue Öyster Cult originate ?
   - a. Denmark
   - b. Germany
   - c. the U.S.

****

2. How did Queen's Freddie Mercury die ?
   - a. from a heart attack
   - b. from AIDS
   - c. he was hit by a delivery van

****

3. Daryl Hall & John Oates became the most successful duo in the history of rock & roll, with more #1 hits than any other rock two-some. Which duo did they surpass for this honor ?
   - a. the Everly Brothers
   - b. Sonny & Cher
   - c. Simon & Garfunkel

****

4. What mid-'70s group was formed from the early-'70s British group the Move ?
   - a. Electric Light Orchestra
   - b. Thin Lizzy
   - c. T. Rex

5. According to the Billboard Hot 100 singles chart, what was the most successful song for Sire Records during the '70s & '80s ?

      a. *Pop Muzik*

      b. *Like a Virgin*

      c. *Back On the Chain Gang*

****

6. What was the #1 U.S. Billboard chart single from the entire decade of the '70s ?

      a. *You Light Up My Life* / Debby Boone

      b. *Bridge Over Troubled Water* / Simon & Garfunkel

      c. *Joy to the World* / Three Dog Night

****

7. Who is the only female singer in the '50s–'80s to have three consecutive #1 albums ?

      a. Madonna

      b. Olivia Newton-John

      c. Donna Summer

****

8. Which group featured members including Glenn, David and Beeb ?

      a. the Eagles

      b. Boston

      c. the Little River Band

9. In what movie did Rose Royce's 1977 hit *I Wanna Get Next To You* appear ?

> a. *Superfly*
>
> b. *The Mandingo*
>
> c. *Car Wash*

****

10. What was Aerosmith leader Steven Tyler's real (birth) name ?

> a. Jason Tyler
>
> b. Stephen Tyler
>
> c. Steven Talarico

****

Questions 11-16: SONG HITS

11. What was Boston's first single to reach the U.S. Billboard Top 20 record charts ?

> a. *Amanda*
>
> b. *More Than a Feeling*
>
> c. *Don't Look Back*

****

12. What was the Four Tops' last U.S. Top 40 hit ?

> a. *When She Was My Girl*
>
> b. *Ain't No Woman (Like the One I've Got)*
>
> c. *Sweet Understanding Love*

13. What was Journey's first Top 20 hit single ?

     a. *Who's Crying Now*

     b. *Lovin', Touchin', Squeezin'*

     c. *Don't Stop Believing*

****

14. Which of the following hits charted highest for the Little River Band on the U.S. Billboard singles chart ?

     a. *Reminiscing*

     b. *Lonesome Loser*

     c. *Lady*

****

15. What was Chic's first U.S. Billboard Top 40 hit ?

     a. *Le Freak*

     b. *Dance, Dance, Dance (Yowsah, Yowsah, Yowsah)*

     c. *Good Times*

****

16. What was Frankie Valli's last solo U.S. Top 40 hit ?

     a. *Our Day Will Come*

     b. *Grease*

     c. *Fallen Angel*

17. In which '60s band was Larry Graham, whose single *One In a Million You* reached #9 on the singles chart in 1980, the bass player ?

      a. the Originals

      b. Sly & the Family Stone

      c. the American Breed

****

18. Where did Daryl Hall and John Oates first meet ?

      a. on the set of a horror movie

      b. in the ocean, being among those rescued in the throes of a strong rip current

      c. in an elevator, escaping a gang fight

****

19. Which '70s singer appeared on *the Merv Griffin Show* and on *Shindig* with his face covered by a ski mask, singing as "The Covered Man" ?

      a. Paul Davis

      b. Billy Joel

      c. David Soul

****

20. Which rock star made the following comment in a 1976 interview: "I never wanted to do this in the first place. I only wanted to be a songwriter . . ." ?

      a. Elton John

      b. Rod Stewart

      c. Paul Simon

answers

Quiz 14

1. c. the U.S., the Ö added for international appeal
2. b. from AIDS, in 1991
3. a. the Everly Brothers
4. a. Electric Light Orchestra, both groups featuring Jeff Lynne as lead singer
5. b. *Like a Virgin,* by Madonna
6. a. *You Light Up My Life* / Debby Boone
7. c. Donna Summer
8. c. the Little River Band
9. c. *Car Wash*
10. c. Steven Talarico

****

Questions 11-16: SONG HITS

11. b. *More Than a Feeling,* in 1976
12. a. *When She Was My Girl,* in 1981
13. b. *Lovin', Touchin', Squeezin',* in 1979
14. a. *Reminiscing,* reaching #3 in 1978
15. b. *Dance, Dance, Dance (Yowsah, Yowsah, Yowsah)*
16. b. *Grease*

****

Questions 17-20: HARDER QUESTIONS

17. b. Sly & the Family Stone
18. c. in a service elevator while trying to escape a brawl between rival gangs which had broken out at the Adelphi Ballroom in Philadelphia
19. c. David Soul, later known for his 1977 hit, *Don't Give Up On Us* alongside his role as Detective Ken Hutchinson in the television series *Starsky & Hutch*
20. a. Elton John, in a 1976 *Rolling Stone* interview

Quiz 15

1. Who was the singer on Grover Washington's 1981 hit *Just the Two Of Us*?

      a. Luther Ingram
      b. Bill Withers
      c. Bill Medley

****

2. Who wrote Kenny Rogers' #1 1980 hit *Lady*?

      a. Barry Manilow
      b. Lionel Richie
      c. Paul Anka

****

3. What '60s group was led by Whitney Houston's mother, Cissy Houston?

      a. the Jaynetts
      b. the Flirtations
      c. the Sweet Inspirations

****

4. Which of the following hits was NOT from Men At Work's first album?

      a. *Overkill*
      b. *Who Can It Be Now*
      c. *Down Under*

5. Which group featured members including Graham, David, Criston, and Russell ?

       a. Air Supply

       b. REO Speedwagon

       c. the Little River Band

****

6. On which label did Heart record their hits *Magic Man* and *Crazy On You* ?

       a. Mushroom

       b. Portrait

       c. Epic

****

7. In what movie did Johnny Lee's 1980 hit *Lookin' for Love* appear ?

       a. *Summer Lovers*

       b. *A Small Circle of Friends*

       c. *Urban Cowboy*

****

8. Who won the Grammy for Best New Artist of the Year for 1980 ?

       a. Pat Benatar

       b. Irene Cara

       c. Christopher Cross

9. Which group featured members including Dave and Annie ?

        a. the Motels

        b. the Eurythmics

        c. DeBarge

****

10. Rogers Nelson was the real (birth) name for which of the following singers ?

        a. Marvin Gaye

        b. Prince

        c. Rod Stewart

****

11. In what movie did Electric Light Orchestra's 1980 hits *All Over the World* and *I'm Alive* appear ?

        a. *Blues Brothers*

        b. *Serial*

        c. *Xanadu*

****

12. Which group featured members including Robert, Tom, Rick and Bun E. ?

        a. Styx

        b. Cheap Trick

        c. the Cars

Questions 13-16: SONG HITS

****

13. Which of the following hits charted highest for Rick Springfield on the U.S. Billboard singles chart ?

> a. *Don't Talk to Strangers*
>
> b. *Jessie's Girl*
>
> c. *Love Somebody*

****

14. Of their six #1 hits, which one stayed on top the longest for Daryl Hall and John Oates ?

> a. *Maneater*
>
> b. *Kiss on My List*
>
> c. *Rich Girl*

****

15. Foreigner's *I Want to Know What Love Is* spent two weeks in the #1 position. What Foreigner song spent ten weeks in the #2 position three years earlier ?

> a. *Hot Blooded*
>
> b. *Double Vision*
>
> c. *Waiting For a Girl Like You*

****

16. Blondie had four #1 hits. Which one was #1 for the longest period of time ?

> a. *Call Me*
>
> b. *Heart of Glass*
>
> c. *Rapture*

17. Which of the following groups was Bruce Springsteen NOT a member of ?

                    a. Earth
                    b. Child
                    c. Comet

****

18. What was the first James Bond theme to reach #1 on the U.S. singles chart ?

                    a. *A View to a Kill*
                    b. *Nobody Does It Better*
                    c. *Live and Let Die*

****

19. Who was the first Western group to perform in Bombay, India ?

                    a. the Police
                    b. Journey
                    c. Foreigner

****

20. Who was described in a newspaper review as generating "the kind of hysteria I haven't heard since the Beatles tore across the opening frames of *A Hard Day's Night . . .*" ?

                    a. Bruce Springsteen
                    b. Prince
                    c. David Bowie

answers

Quiz 15

1. b. Bill Withers
2. b. Lionel Richie
3. c. the Sweet Inspirations
4. a. *Overkill*
5. a. Air Supply
6. a. Mushroom
7. c. *Urban Cowboy*
8. c. Christopher Cross
9. b. the Eurythmics
10. b. Prince (full name: Prince Rogers Nelson)
11. c. *Xanadu*
12. b. Cheap Trick

****

Questions 13-16: SONG HITS

13. b. *Jessie's Girl*, #1 for 2 weeks in 1981
14. a. *Maneater*, #1 for four weeks in 1982
15. c. *Waiting For a Girl Like You*, which got upstaged by Olivia Newton-John's *Physical* for most of its reign in 1981
16. a. *Call Me*, #1 for six weeks in 1980

****

Questions 17-20: HARDER QUESTIONS

17. c. Comet
18. a. *A View to a Kill*, by Duran Duran in 1985 . . . the other two only reached #2
19. a. the Police, on March 25, 1980
20. b. Prince, in a review of the movie *Purple Rain*

Quiz 16

1. What unusual "instrument" did producer Greg Perry play on Dolly Parton's 1981 hit *9 to 5*?
   - a. a typewriter
   - b. a washboard
   - c. a musical comb

****

2. What inspired Lionel Richie's song *Three Times a Lady*?
   - a. his wife
   - b. his parents
   - c. a musical variety show

****

3. What famous early '60s star did Bruce Springsteen produce during the early '80s?
   - a. Ben E. King
   - b. Roy Orbison
   - c. Gary U.S. Bonds

****

4. Who sang backup vocals on Christopher Cross's 1980 hit *Ride Like the Wind*?
   - a. Michael McDonald
   - b. Glenn Frey
   - c. Phil Collins

5. For what word is the name Devo a shortened form ?

        a. "devour"

        b. "de-evolution"

        c. "redevelopment"

****

6. What was the real (birth) name of J. Geils lead singer Peter Wolf ?

        a. Peter Wolfsson

        b. Petrovich Manikopf

        c. Peter Blankfield

****

7. In what 1982 movie did Jackson Browne's *Somebody's Baby* appear in ?

        a. *Private Lessons*

        b. *Fast Times at Ridgemont High*

        c. *Porky's*

****

8. Which single won a Grammy for Record of the Year for 1981?

        a. *Bette Davis Eyes*

        b. *Endless Love*

        c. *Physical*

9. Which group featured members including Joe, Rick, Steve and Phil ?

        a. the Cars

        b. the Steve Miller Band

        c. Def Leppard

****

10. What 1985 hit was the love theme for the movie *White Nights* ?

        a. *Separate Lives*

        b. *The Power of Love*

        c. *We Don't Need Another Hero*

****

11. What was the real (birth) name of Queen leader Freddie Mercury ?

        a. Fred McLendon

        b. Georgio Mercurio

        c. Frederick Bulsara

****

12. On which label did the Pat Benatar record her hits, including *Hit Me With Your Best Shot* ?

        a. Chrysalis

        b. Liberty

        c. Planet

Questions 13-16: SONG HITS

```
**************************************************
```

13. What was the Eurythmics' first U.S. Billboard
Top 40 hit ?

    a. *Would I Lie To You ?*

    b. *Sweet Dreams (Are Made Of This)*

    c. *Here Comes the Rain Again*

```
**************************************************
```

14. Which of the following #1 hits charted the longest
for Prince on the U.S. Billboard singles chart ?

    a. *When Doves Cry*

    b. *Let's Go Crazy*

    c. *Kiss*

```
**************************************************
```

15. Which of the following hits charted highest for
Billy Ocean on the U.S. Billboard singles chart ?

    a. *Suddenly*

    b. *Caribbean Queen*

    c. *There'll Be Sad Songs (To Make You Cry)*

```
**************************************************
```

16. What was Marvin Gaye's last U.S. Top 40 hit ?

    a. *Got to Give It Up*

    b. *Sexual Healing*

    c. *Let's Get It On*

17. What was the original title that Rick Springfield considered before changing the lyrics and the title of his 1981 song to *Jessie's Girl* ?

> a. *Jerry's Girl*
> b. *Another Girl*
> c. *Gary's Girl*

****

18. Who was originally asked to sing the song *Call Me*, the #1 hit for Blondie in 1980 ?

> a. Olivia Newton-John
> b. Diana Ross
> c. Stevie Nicks

****

19. Which of the following 1981 songs was banned by some radio stations for causing "an uncomfortableness among listeners" ?

> a. *Start Me Up*
> b. *Rapture*
> c. *Physical*

****

20. Who was *Rolling Stone Magazine* contributor Jon Landau referring to when he wrote in 1974: "I saw rock and roll's future" ?

> a. Bruce Springsteen
> b. Barry Manilow
> c. Bee Gees

Quiz 16

1. a. a typewriter
2. b. his parents — at their 37th wedding anniversary, where sentiments of gratitude inspired Richie's song
3. c. Gary U.S. Bonds
4. a. Michael McDonald
5. b. "de-evolution", the band's commentary on the status of mankind
6. c. Peter Blankfield
7. b. *Fast Times at Ridgemont High*
8. a. *Bette Davis Eyes,* by Kim Carnes
9. c. Def Leppard
10. a. *Separate Lives,* sung by Phil Collins & Marilyn Martin
11. c. Frederick Bulsara
12. a. Chrysalis

****

Questions 13-16: SONG HITS

13. b. *Sweet Dreams (Are Made Of This)*
14. a. *When Doves Cry,* #1 for 5 weeks in 1984
15. b. *Caribbean Queen,* #1 for 2 weeks in 1984
16. b. *Sexual Healing,* in 1983

****

Questions 17-20: HARDER QUESTIONS

17. c. *Gary's Girl* . . . the song was actually written about his friend's girlfriend
18. c. Stevie Nicks, who turned down the offer
19. c. *Physical* . . . Due to its double-entendre, several "easy-listening" stations left it out of its rotation
20. a. Bruce Springsteen, after Landau first saw Springsteen perform live on stage

Quiz 17

1. Which famous British rocker added vocals — and his own melody — to Dire Straits' biggest hit, *Money for Nothing* ?

     a. Elton John

     b. Billy Idol

     c. Sting

****

2. Who sang along with Luther Ingram on his 1984 hit *Yah Mo B There* ?

     a. Bill Withers

     b. Peabo Bryson

     c. Michael McDonald

****

3. After what were Dexys Midnight Runners named ?

     a. dexedrine

     b. the manager's pet hamster

     c. an early–'40s cowboy movie

****

4. Rockwell, artist with the 1984 hit *Somebody's Watching Me,* used a pseudonym to avoid association with his music-icon dad. Who was Rockwell's dad ?

     a. Nat "King" Cole

     b. Berry Gordy, Jr.

     c. Quincy Jones

5. In what 1985 movie did Huey Lewis & the News' hit
The Power of Love appear ?

        a. *The Coca-Cola Kid*

        b. *The Woman in Red*

        c. *Back to the Future*

****

6. What was '80s singer Shannon's real (birth) name ?

        a. Sharon Delacorte

        b. Shannon Smith

        c. Brenda Greene

****

7. On which label did the Police record their hits,
including *Every Breath You Take* ?

        a. A&M

        b. Geffen

        c. Millennium

****

8. Who won the Grammy for Best New Artist of the
Year for 1982 ?

        a. John Cougar (Mellencamp)

        b. Men At Work

        c. Musical Youth

9. Which group featured members including Curt and Roland ?

        a. Toto

        b. Boston

        c. Tears for Fears

****

10. In what movie did Olivia Newton-John's 1984 hit *Twist of Fate* appear ?

        a. *The Honorary Consul*

        b. *Two of a Kind*

        c. *Best Friends*

****

11. What was the real (birth) name of Jon Bon Jovi ?

        a. Jon DeGiovanni

        b. Ron Cachetti

        c. John Bongiovi

****

12. Which group featured members including Jimmy, Robert, Jeff and Paul ?

        a. Duran Duran

        b. the Honeydrippers

        c. the Traveling Wilburys

Questions 13-16: **SONG HITS**

****

13. Which of the following hits charted highest for Toto on the U.S. Billboard singles chart ?

        a. *Hold the Line*

        b. *Rosanna*

        c. *Africa*

****

14. What was Billy Idol's first Top 20 hit ?

        a. *Eyes Without a Face*

        b. *White Wedding*

        c. *Rebel Yell*

****

15. Which of the following #1 hits charted the longest for Madonna on the U.S. Billboard singles chart ?

        a. *Live to Tell*

        b. *Like a Virgin*

        c. *Papa Don't Preach*

****

16. What was Cyndi Lauper's first U.S. #1 hit ?

        a. *Time After Time*

        b. *True Colors*

        c. *Girls Just Want to Have Fun*

17. Which band did Rick Springfield NOT once play with ?

      a. the Comfortable Chair

      b. Zoot

      c. Wackedy Wak

****

18. The origin of the group name Toto has been an enduring mystery. Which of the following was NOT a reason for the band's choice of their name ?

      a. it was from a Latin phrase

      b. it was inspired by *The Wizard of Oz*

      c. it came from lead singer Bobby Kimball's original last name, Toteaux

****

19. With what band did Phil Collins play as a teenager, recording an album in the process ?

      a. the London Berries

      b. Flaming Youth

      c. Cosmic Transformation

****

20. Who was described as a "Bible-reading health food devotee who sang of religion and sex" ?

      a. Prince

      b. Rod Stewart

      c. George Michael

Quiz 17

1. c. Sting, who interjected the words "I Want My MTV" to the melody of *Don't Stand So Close to Me*
2. c. Michael McDonald
3. a. dexedrine, a widely used "upper" drug
4. b. Berry Gordy, Jr. — besides recording on his Motown–founder dad's label, Kennedy "Rockwell" Gordy also boasted backup vocals by another Motown star: Michael Jackson
5. c. *Back to the Future*
6. c. Brenda Shannon Greene
7. a. A&M
8. b. Men At Work
9. c. Tears for Fears
10. b. *Two of a Kind*
11. c. John Bongiovi
12. b. the Honeydrippers

****

Questions 13-16: SONG HITS

13. c. *Africa*, #1 in 1983
14. a. *Eyes Without a Face*
15. b. *Like a Virgin*, #1 for 6 weeks in 1984
16. a. *Time After Time* . . . although released earlier, *Girls Just Want to Have Fun* only reached #2

****

Questions 17-20: HARDER QUESTIONS

17. a. the Comfortable Chair
18. c. though oft–mentioned as "fact", the "Toteaux" rumor was just that, a rumor floated by the bandmembers themselves, profferred merely in jest . . .
19. b. Flaming Youth, recording the album *Ark 2*
20. a. Prince

Quiz 18

1. Men at Work popularized the vegemite sandwich in their 1982 hit *Down Under.* What is vegemite ?

    a. an herbal vegetable

    b. a peppered spice

    c. a salty yeast spread

****

2. What 1964 minor hit song did the Rolling Stones record and take all the way to #5 in 1986 ?

    a. *Going to a Go-Go*

    b. *Ain't Too Proud to Beg*

    c. *Harlem Shuffle*

****

3. In 1965, Petula Clark became the first female vocalist to have her first two singles place in the Top 3 in the U.S. Which female star topped this feat in 1984 ?

    a. Madonna

    b. Tina Turner

    c. Cyndi Lauper

****

4. What was the name of Bruce Springsteen's long-running backup group ?

    a. the Sonic Boom

    b. the E Street Band

    c. the Asbury Dukes

5. According to the Billboard Hot 100 singles chart, what was the most successful song for Island Records during the '70s & '80s ?

 a. *Up Where We Belong*

 b. *With Or Without You*

 c. *Addicted to Love*

****

6. On which label did Madonna record her biggest hits, including *Material Girl* ?

 a. Sire

 b. Geffen

 c. De-Lite

****

7. In what 1985 movie did Force M.D.'s song *Tender Love* appear ?

 a. *Blue Velvet*

 b. *Krush Groove*

 c. *Short Circuit*

****

8. According to Billboard's Hot 100 singles chart, what was the #1 song for 1986 ?

 a. *Walk Like An Egyptian*

 b. *You Give Love a Bad Name*

 c. *That's What Friends Are For*

9. Which group featured members including Sammy, Michael, David and Eddie ?

        a. Van Halen

        b. Dire Straits

        c. Simple Minds

****

10. On which label did the Pet Shop Boys record their hits, including *West End Girls* ?

        a. EMI America

        b. Polydor

        c. Liberty

****

11. Who replaced lead singer David Lee Roth shortly after his departure from Van Halen ?

        a. Jon Bon Jovi

        b. Sammy Hagar

        c. Alex Van Halen

****

12. What Top 5 Survivor hit came from the movie *Rocky IV* ?

        a. *Burning Heart*

        b. *The Search is Over*

        c. *I Can't Hold Back*

Questions 13-16: **SONG HITS**

****

13. What was Queen's last U.S. Top 40 hit ?

     a. *Another One Bites the Dust*

     b. *Body Language*

     c. *Radio Ga-Ga*

****

14. What was Kim Carnes' first U.S. Billboard Top 40 hit ?

     a. *Draw Of the Cards*

     b. *More Love*

     c. *Bette Davis Eyes*

****

15. Which of the following #1 hits charted the longest for Phil Collins on the U.S. Billboard singles chart ?

     a. *Against All Odds (Take a Look At Me Now)*

     b. *One More Night*

     c. *Sussudio*

****

16. What was Corey Hart's first U.S. Billboard Top 40 hit ?

     a. *Never Surrender*

     b. *Sunglasses At Night*

     c. *Boy In the Box*

17. What song by Daryl Hall & John Oates, their 12th Top 10 Billboard hit, made them the most successful duo in U.S. rock history ?

> a. *Kiss On My List*
>
> b. *One on One*
>
> c. *Say It Isn't So*

****

18. The Whispers had a 1987 hit *Rock Steady* — but what is "Rock Steady" ?

> a. a modern dance
>
> b. a form of reggae
>
> c. an expression of solidarity

****

19. Who provided the background vocals for Billy Joel's 1984 hit *The Longest Time* ?

> a. Billy Joel
>
> b. Sha Na Na
>
> c. the Jordainaires

****

20. What was unique about Toni Basil's 1982 hit *Mickey*?

> a. it was recorded during the half-time of a high school football game
>
> b. it was the first video played on MTV
>
> c. it featured actual cheerleaders

answers

Quiz 18

1. c. a salty yeast spread
2. c. *Harlem Shuffle,* which reached #44 for Bob & Earl in 1964
3. c. Cyndi Lauper, who had her first three singles reach the Top 3
4. b. the E Street Band
5. a. *Up Where We Belong,* by Joe Cocker & Jennifer Warnes
6. a. Sire
7. b. *Krush Groove*
8. c. *That's What Friends Are For,* by Dionne & Friends
9. a. Van Halen
10. a. EMI America
11. b. Sammy Hagar, lead singer of lesser-known '80s band Montrose
12. a. *Burning Heart*

****

Questions 13-16: SONG HITS

13. c. *Radio Ga-Ga,* in 1984
14. b. *More Love*
15. a. *Against All Odds (Take a Look At Me Now),* #1 for 3 weeks
    in 1984
16. b. *Sunglasses At Night*

****

Questions 17-20: HARDER QUESTIONS

17. c. *Say It Isn't So,* which pushed them past the Everly Brothers
    in 1983 as the #1 all-time rock duo
18. b. a form of reggae — In the 1960s, Jamaican music known
    as "ska" was fast-paced . . . from it emerged a slower-paced
    form, called "Rock Steady", which later evolved into "reggae"
19. a. *all* voices and harmonies were sung by Billy Joel himself!
20. c. it featured the Los Angeles' Dorsey High School
    cheerleaders alongside her . . . Toni Basil had actually
    been the former head cheerleader of her own high school
    in Las Vegas

Quiz 19

1. Who provided backup vocals on Eddie Money's 1986 hit *Take Me Home Tonight* ?
   - a. Bonnie Tyler
   - b. Ronnie Spector
   - c. Tina Turner

****

2. In what movie did Kenny Loggins' 1986 hit *(Highway to the) Danger Zone* appear ?
   - a. *Year of the Dragon*
   - b. *Top Gun*
   - c. *Colors*

****

3. Who was Diana Ross's 1985 hit *Missing You* a tribute to ?
   - a. Jackie Wilson
   - b. her father
   - c. Marvin Gaye

****

4. In the "rap" world, what does "down" mean, as in a "down dude" ?
   - a. rich and powerful
   - b. independent
   - c. lazy

5. What was the actual name of *99 Luftballons* singer Nena ?

    a. Shirley Johansson

    b. Bernadette McNair

    c. Gabriele Kerner

****

6. In what 1987 movie did the Chordettes' 1958 hit *Lollipop* appear ?

    a. *Stand By Me*

    b. *Outrageous Fortune*

    c. *The Secret Of My Success*

****

7. Which group featured members including Izzy, Duff and Slash ?

    a. INXS

    b. Guns N' Roses

    c. the Pet Shop Boys

****

8. Who won the Grammy for Best New Artist of the Year for 1988 ?

    a. Debbie Gibson

    b. White Lion

    c. Tracy Chapman

9. In what movie did Lionel Richie's 1985 hit *Say You, Say Me* appear ?

>   a. *White Nights*
>   b. *The Woman In Red*
>   c. *Teen Wolf*

****

10. On which label did Cyndi Lauper record her hits, including *Girls Just Want to Have Fun* ?

>   a. Portrait
>   b. Arista
>   c. Planet

****

11. Who sang lead on Van Halen's 1986 hit *Why Can't This Be Love* ?

>   a. Sammy Hagar
>   b. David Lee Roth
>   c. Eddie Van Halen

****

12. In what 1986 movie did New Edition's revival of the Penguins' 1955 hit *Earth Angel* appear ?

>   a. *Pretty in Pink*
>   b. *Stand By Me*
>   c. *The Karate Kid Part II*

Questions 13-16: **SONG HITS**

****

13. What was Huey Lewis & the News' first single to reach the U.S. Billboard Top 20 record charts ?

     a. *Do You Believe In Love*

     b. *Heart and Soul*

     c. *I Want a New Drug*

****

14. What was Tears For Fears' first U.S. Billboard Top 40 hit ?

     a. *Shout*

     b. *Head Over Heels*

     c. *Everybody Wants to Rule the World*

****

15. Which of the following #1 hits charted the longest for Olivia Newton-John on the U.S. Billboard singles chart ?

     a. *I Honestly Love You*

     b. *Magic*

     c. *Physical*

****

16. What was Bruce Springsteen's first single to reach the U.S. Billboard Top 20 record charts ?

     a. *Dancing In the Dark*

     b. *Born In the U.S.A.*

     c. *I'm On Fire*

HARDER QUESTIONS (17-20): 2 points each
(4 points if you can answer the question without the three choices !)

17. Elton John and Stevie Wonder had recorded albums which debuted at #1 on the U.S. chart. The next to accomplish this feat was Bruce Springsteen, in 1986. But what was unusual about Springsteen's album ?

    a. it was a 5-LP-set

    b. it contained no Top 40 single hits

    c. the album tracks were not listed

****

18. "Heart" was shortened from their previous name. What was it ?

    a. Broken Heart

    b. White Heart

    c. Heart and Soul

****

19. Which rock group did Dire Straits tour with during their first U.K. gig ?

    a. the Rolling Stones

    b. the Clash

    c. Talking Heads

****

20. Which '80s rocker was inspired to become a drummer when he first heard the 1963 Surfaris hit, *Wipe Out* ?

    a. Phil Collins

    b. Eddie Van Halen

    c. Sting

Quiz 19

1. b. Ronnie Spector, who reprised her popular *Be My Baby* tune
2. b. *Top Gun,* starring Tom Cruise
3. c. Marvin Gaye
4. b. independent
5. c. Gabriele Kerner
6. a. *Stand By Me*
7. b. Guns N' Roses . . . as well as leader Axl Rose
8. c. Tracy Chapman
9. a. *White Nights*
10. a. Portrait
11. a. Sammy Hagar
12. c. *The Karate Kid Part II*

****

Questions 13-16: SONG HITS

13. a. *Do You Believe In Love,* in 1982
14. c. *Everybody Wants to Rule the World*
15. c. *Physical,* #1 for 10 weeks in 1981
16. a. *Dancing In the Dark,* in June, 1984

****

Questions 17-20: HARDER QUESTIONS

17. a. *Bruce Springsteen & the E Street Band* was a 5-LP box-set
18. b. White Heart
19. c. Talking Heads
20. b. Eddie Van Halen . . . as it turned out, his brother Alex played his drum-set better than he could, so he turned to guitar . . . the music world is grateful that he did !

Quiz 20

1. Who sang on Herb Alpert's 1987 hit *Diamonds* ?
   a. Paula Abdul
   b. Jody Watley
   c. Janet Jackson

****

2. Two different albums from the '80s each spawned seven U.S. Top 10 singles. Which album was NOT one of them ?
   a. *Overkill*
   b. *Thriller*
   c. *Born In the U.S.A.*

****

3. What term was applied to groups such as Kiss and Twisted Sister ?
   a. Acid-Rock
   b. Punk-Rock
   c. Glam-Rock

****

4. Who provided backing vocals on Dionne Warwick's 1983 hit *Heartbreaker* ?
   a. Neil Sedaka
   b. Smokey Robinson
   c. Barry Gibb

5. On which label did Bryan Adams record his hits, including *Run to You* ?

        a. A&M

        b. Elektra

        c. Grunt

****

6. Leslie Sebastian Charles was the real (birth) name for which of the following singers ?

        a. Lionel Richie

        b. Billy Joel

        c. Billy Ocean

****

7. In what movie did Madonna's 1985 hit *Crazy For You* appear ?

        a. *The Coca-Cola Kid*

        b. *The Heavenly Kid*

        c. *Vision Quest*

****

8. Who won the Grammy for Best New Artist of the Year for 1987 ?

        a. U2

        b. Jody Watley

        c. Los Lobos

9. Which group featured members including Vicki, Debbi and Susanna ?

        a. the Bangles

        b. the Go-Go's

        c. Exposé

****

10. What heavy-metal group was Dee Snider lead singer for ?

        a. Iron Maiden

        b. Twisted Sister

        c. AC/DC

****

11. Which of the following songs was NOT featured in *Rocky IV* ?

        a. *Don't Lose My Number* / Phil Collins

        b. *Living in America* / James Brown

        c. *Burning Heart* / Survivor

****

12. Which group featured members including Ricky, Bobby, Ralph and Michael ?

        a. the Pet Shop Boys

        b. New Edition

        c. the Boys Club

Questions 13-16: **SONG HITS**

****

13. What was Wham!'s first U.S. Billboard Top 40 hit ?

    a. *Wake Me Up Before You Go-Go*

    b. *Everything She Wants*

    c. *Careless Whisper*

****

14. What was Prince's first single to reach the U.S. Billboard Top 20 record charts ?

    a. *I Wanna Be Your Lover*

    b. *Little Red Corvette*

    c. *Raspberry Beret*

****

15. What was Whitney Houston's first U.S. #1 hit ?

    a. *Saving All My Love For You*

    b. *Greatest Love Of All*

    c. *How Will I Know*

****

16. What was Don Henley's first solo U.S. Billboard Top 40 hit ?

    a. *The Boys of Summer*

    b. *Dirty Laundry*

    c. *All She Wants To Do Is Dance*

HARDER QUESTIONS (17-20): 2 points each
(4 points if you can answer the question without the three choices !)

17. Which of the following was NOT a former band name for the members of Cheap Trick ?

        a. Fuse

        b. Chicken Funk

        c. Sick Man of Europe

****

18. Who was the actual singer of the 1985 Christmas parody of Elvis Presley's *Blue Christmas* ?

        a. Ray Stevens

        b. Denny Brownlee

        c. Seymour Swine

****

19. Who provided backing vocals on Foreigner's 1985 hit *I Want to Know What Love Is* ?

        a. the Northern California State Youth Choir

        b. the Philadelphia Boys Choir

        c. the New Jersey Mass Choir

****

20. Bing Crosby's *White Christmas* was the biggest-selling single of all time. What was the second best-selling single in history ?

        a. *Hey Jude*

        b. *Candle in the Wind*

        c. *Billie Jean*

a n s w e r s

Quiz 20

1. c. Janet Jackson
2. a. *Overkill*
3. c. Glam-Rock
4. c. Barry Gibb
5. a. A&M
6. c. Billy Ocean
7. c. *Vision Quest*
8. b. Jody Watley
9. a. the Bangles
10. b. Twisted Sister
11. a. *Don't Lose My Number* / Phil Collins
12. b. New Edition

****

Questions 13-16: SONG HITS

13. a. *Wake Me Up Before You Go-Go*
14. a. *I Wanna Be Your Lover,* in 1980
15. a. *Saving All My Love For You*
16. b. *Dirty Laundry*

****

Questions 17-20: HARDER QUESTIONS

17. b. Chicken Funk
18. b. Denny Brownlee . . . Ray Stevens recorded a version in 2012 . . . some labels list Mel Blanc and Seymour Swine as artists, but the actual version — which was recorded in 1984 in a local club, only to gain national enthusiasm a year later — was actually sung by the virtually unknown Denny Brownlee
19. c. the New Jersey Mass Choir
20. b. *Candle in the Wind,* Elton John's live performance in honor and memory of Princess Diana, produced by George Martin

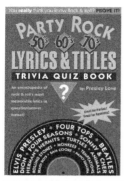

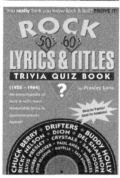
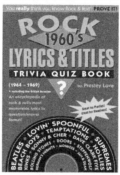
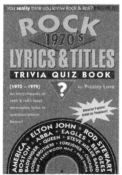
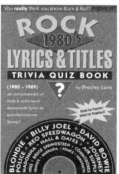

Available on Amazon.com

Printed in Great Britain
by Amazon

81378671R00078